MEMORY LANE

Oh, You Beautiful Doll

SONG
WORDS BY
SEYMOUR BROWN
5

MUSIC BY
NAT D. AYER

JEROME H. REMICK & CO.

NEW·YORK·DETROIT

MEMORY LANE

1890 to 1925

Ragtime, Jazz,
Foxtrot and other
popular music and music covers
Selected by Max Wilk

STVDIOART

11₆54

First published in Great Britain by
Studio International Publications Ltd.,
14 West Central Street, London WC1A 1JH

Copyright © 1973 Optimums Inc and Studio International
Publications Ltd.

The publishers wish to acknowledge the considerable assistance of
M. Jean-Christophe Averty, dedicated afficianado and collector of American
music and records, without whose collection *Memory Lane* could not have
been compiled.

Reproduction of *Ta-Ra-Ra Boom-De-Ay!* is by kind permission of the
Mander and Mitcheson Theatre Collection

ISBN: 0 902063 13 8 paper
0 902063 14 6 cloth

Printed in Great Britain by
W & J Mackay Limited, Chatham, Kent

Introduction

by Max Wilk

Pity our ancestors who lived out their simple lives six or seven decades ago. Six long days was their work week; travel beyond the end of town limits was expensive and inconvenient. Sunday was devoted to church and the major meal of the week. Not for them were the joys of daytime serials, or quiz shows, of Senate investigations, hard-core pornography, commercials selling beer and living girdles, no Lana Turner, no Liberace or Lone Ranger. They were truly a deprived generation.

But it is when we consider the contemporary pre-World War 1 musical scene that we are confronted with true primitivism. Imagine, if you can, an entire culture struggling through life bereft of such absolute necessities as hi-fi, stereo, diamond styli, tape-decks, waffle-speakers and long-play cassettes. Painful, isn't it?

How can we ever hope to experience the utter barrenness of a life-style that for its music depended upon such primitive devices as the banjo, or the upright piano—with the only accessory available being ten human fingers and two feet, with which to press the foot pedals? How curiously pathetic is the picture of all those simple folk of years ago, whiling away their precious leisure hours standing around that piano, trying to make communication with their fellow man and/or woman through the inadequate medium of the unamplified human voice. And what can one feel but compassion for the young blade who wished to serenade a young lady, and had for his basic equipment only his ardour, perhaps a ukelele, and a printed love ballad he'd purchased for ten cents at his local Woolworth's?

For it was that same ballad, that popular song—a unique form of lower-class lieder that was the primary form of culture of that era. Where did they originate? Usually from a section of Manhattan known as Tin Pan Alley. There, in tiny cubbyholes, various gents with various talents kept busy at their pianos, daily turning out melodies. With the assistance of facile rhymsters known as lyricists, these artisans churned out waltzes, one- and two-steps, ballads and humorous comment on current events. Their output was enormous; their work rather rigid in structure. The usual popular song consisted of a short verse, followed by thirty-two bars of music and lyrics.

Their latest effort committed to music paper, the hopeful song-

5

writers would hurry to the offices of various other men near by who had set themselves up in business (just as hopefully) as publishers. Should these entrepreneurs decide that the new ditty might have some popular appeal (and their guess was heavily loaded with conjecture) contracts were signed and a trifling sum known as an advance against royalties changed hands. Eventually the music and lyrics went to press, complete with a cover designed to catch the eye of the potential buyer; and in a matter of days, there began the process of making the song known to the public.

At best, this exploitation process was strictly hit or miss. To this day, nobody knows what sort of song will catch the public fancy and tickle its ear, or why it will remain engrained in our popular culture. There is not now, nor ever has been, a piece of music and lyrics that can be called, at the outset, a 'sure hit'...and the bankruptcy courts have over the years seen a steady parade of unfortunates who firmly believed they knew how to create one.

So then, in that primitive early era, lacking the wonders of electronic mass communications, how was a song publisher to test the waters? Mainly by hard work and ingenuity. His office staff consisted of energetic piano players, whose job it was to sit in cubicles and demonstrate the firm's latest wares to performers in search of material for their 'acts'. There was also a crew of nimble-witted, jovial 'pluggers', whose job it was to pursue the popular stars of the day, and to induce them, by fair means or foul, to introduce that new song, whether it be in a café, or in a long-vanished institution known as two-a-day vaudeville, or on the stages of the legitimate theatres. Should the star's rendition of the song induce even the barest response from his or her audience, it might only be a matter of days before word-of-mouth began. In his morning mail, the publisher would find orders for copies of the sheet music from local music stores. Girls in 5-and-10's sat at upright pianos in the music department and pounded out renditions of the song by the hour, and if the song eventually became a popular success, its commercial life would be a long and fruitful one.

There are certain truisms that emerged from this process. Very rarely was a good performer ever capable of making a success out of a truly bad song. And it is also a fact that the best piece of popular music and lyrics might languish for years, unheard, until it fell into the hands of the right performer.

Across the pages of this book flash the shades of many great stars of those days–Elsie Janis, Gaby Deslys, Fay Templeton, Sophie Tucker, George M Cohan, Bert Williams, Lew Dockstader, and others. All of them were, in their prime, identified with certain songs that they helped to introduce. But it is safe to say that over the years of the first half of the twentieth century, no single performer was ever as successful and identified with as many different songs, as that young man from Baltimore, the cantor's son who ran away from home to join a touring minstral show, Al Jolson. For years there was a saying in popular music circles–if Jolson couldn't make it into a hit, then nobody could.

Other civilizations have left their mark on cave walls, or in statuary or heroic monuments. Some have left behind chiselled odes on marble or passed on their wisdom through frescoes and decorated church altars. But the first half of our twentieth century will be best remembered by future generations because of its popular songs. And sociologists in

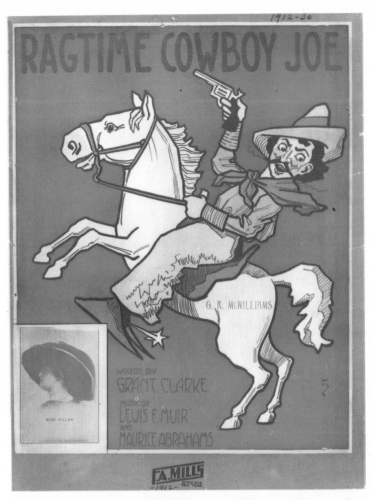

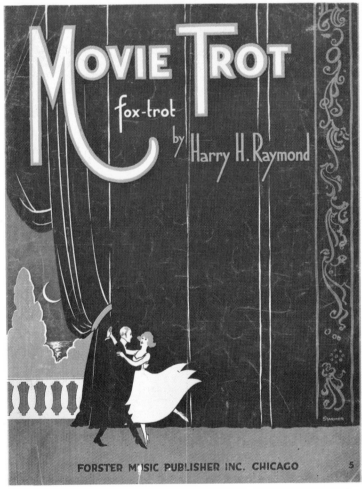

I·NEVER·SAW SUCH·JEALOUSY IN·ALL·MY·LIFE

WORDS·BY·ANDREW·B·STERLING

MUSIC·BY·HARRY·VON·TILZER

HARRY VON TILZER
MUSIC PUBLISHING CO.

THE TWO PUCKS

5

years to come should indeed write interesting PhD theses when they interpret the mores expressed in what was sung and played and strummed in bathtubs, front parlours and barrooms.

The universal subject matter of most of these songs was love. Love in an endless series of permutations, whether it be for a blushing young girl, for a sturdy-muscled father, for a gang of one's old friends, or (most importantly) for one's silver-haired mother. Love was pure; sex was never even hinted at. Marriage was as sturdy an institution as Fort Knox. Married love was celebrated among all the ethnic groups – the Italians, the Irish, the Jewish and the blacks – who in those days were familiarly referred to as the wops, the harps, the hebes and the coons. Love was the great leveler between caste and class. Most of the pressing emotional appeals of the day dealt not with one's politics, or the economy, but with one's girlfriend, the gain or loss of her sweet person. The girl was lovely, she was adorable, she was virtuous and ideal. She danced a lot, she dressed well, she smiled, and the most burning question one could lose sleep over was – if one were forced to leave her, would Miss X still be waiting upon one's return?

Whatever the subject, be it travel, fashion, food, real-estate, or even the latest dance craze – you can be sure that those callous-fingered Tin Pan Alley boys would find some way to tie it up with love. Even great technological advances – the wireless, the telephone, the gasoline engine – all were duly written and sung about, but always in terms of *l'amour*.

Love was born, sustained and cherished in a home. Said home was usually a rustic farmhouse, a vine-covered cottage, or some idealized tumbledown shack. The site of these places might be a rolling sweep of Indiana farmland, or an orange-grove in California, the plains of the Far West, or in 'Dixie'. Dixie can be defined as any piece of ground below the mythical Mason–Dixon Line, and its fields, which belonged to plantations, were inhabited always by jolly fieldhands who picked cotton for massah, laughed while they worked the live-long eleven-hour day until after supper, at which point whey could miraculously summon up sufficient energy to dance the cake-walk and sing the whole night long. Travel to see one's (hopefully) waiting sweetie in Dixie was accomplished by leaping aboard a fast flyer to Florida, or the midnight choo-choo to Alabam', or the 10.10 to Tennessee.

In the early 1900's, hundreds, nay thousands, of these simple ditties were written, published and sold to the populace, which brought them home, spread them out on the piano rack and cheerfully played and sang them to each other. But in the years that followed, Mr Thomas A Edison's invention of the talking-machine, with its cylinders that brought performers' voices into the parlour, began to chip away at the popularity of the published song. By the early 1920's, there appeared the radio; every home became equipped with its own crystal set. On a clear night, one could listen to other voices crooning – from as far away as Bridgeport! Soon, every consumer owned his own Atwater Kent super-heterodyne, and dust began to gather on the closed lid of the family Steinway. By the time 1928 was upon us, with the introduction of the talking-picture, the days of sheet-music had passed. Why should anyone try to compete with Al Jolson singing on a phonograph record, or from the silver screen? The professional performers had taken over.

Nowadays, such sheet music as is published is a mere token of the songwriter's art. Most of it goes into libraries. In order to unearth the yellowing relics of those earlier years, one must search through piano benches, or local rummage-sales, or in Salvation Army warehouses, where such pages were long ago consigned.

This random assemblage of sheet music covers of that long-gone era is not only amusing and pleasant; it serves a sociological purpose. For does it not prove that we have all matured enormously? Instead of worrying about where Robinson Crusoe went with Friday, on Saturday night, we spend our days coping with overpopulation. We couldn't care less who paid the rent for Mrs Rip Van Winkle while her husband slept for forty years; we're far too busy with ecological balances and the pollution of our waters. Consider a naive era in which the only call to stir one's baser chauvinist nature was to point out that if one could fight like one could love, goodnight Germany...and try dropping that notion into the Middle East!

Yes–that early 20th century was a simple-minded time, and we should all be grateful that we have matured into sober, thoughtful, hypertense responsible citizens, only too aware of the problems of surviving on this planet in 1973...and prepared to deal with the potential terrors of tomorrow. Those simple folk of 1909 or so were more to be pitied than censured for their incredible naivete, right? Right on.

...but if that's so, then tell us, Father William, why is it that the simplistic, child-like pop-song world that is mirrored on the ensuing pages of *Memory Lane* seems so damned much more attractive than our own?

DUBLIN DAISIES
INTERMEZZO — TWO STEP
By Percy Wenrich
Composer of Rainbow
JEROME H. REMICK & CO.
5
DETROIT — NEW YORK

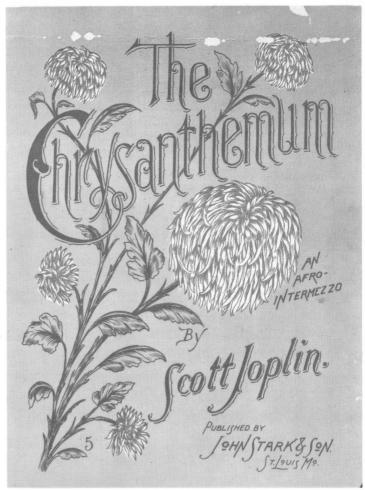

UN SUCCES SANS PRECEDENT
YOU MADE ME LOVE YOU
(i DiDN'T WANT TO DO iT)
DANSE PAR
MiSTiNGUETT
Copyright 1913
For the British Empire (except Canada)
Francis Day and Hunter, London.
For the Continent of Europe Chappell & Co
and Francis Day and Hunter, London.
For the United States of America and Canada
The Broadway Music Corporation New-York.
Publié par arrangement
avec Chappell & Co
et Francis Day and Hunter
PRiX NET : 2 frs
EDiTiONS EDOUARD SALABERT
(FRANCiS SALABERT)
22 RUE CHAUCHAT PARiS

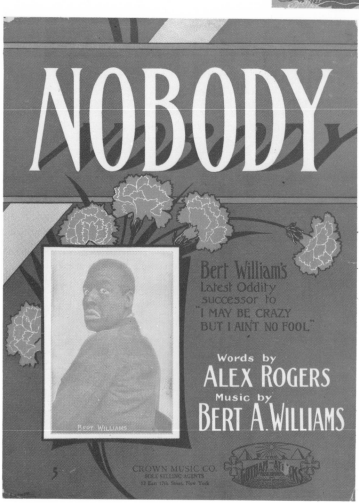

UNDERTAKERS' BLUES

By RAY LOPEZ Writer of LIVERY·STABLE BLUES

ROGER GRAHAM · 143 N.Dearborn, CHICAGO.

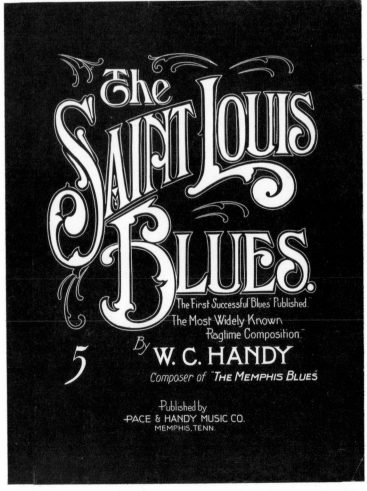

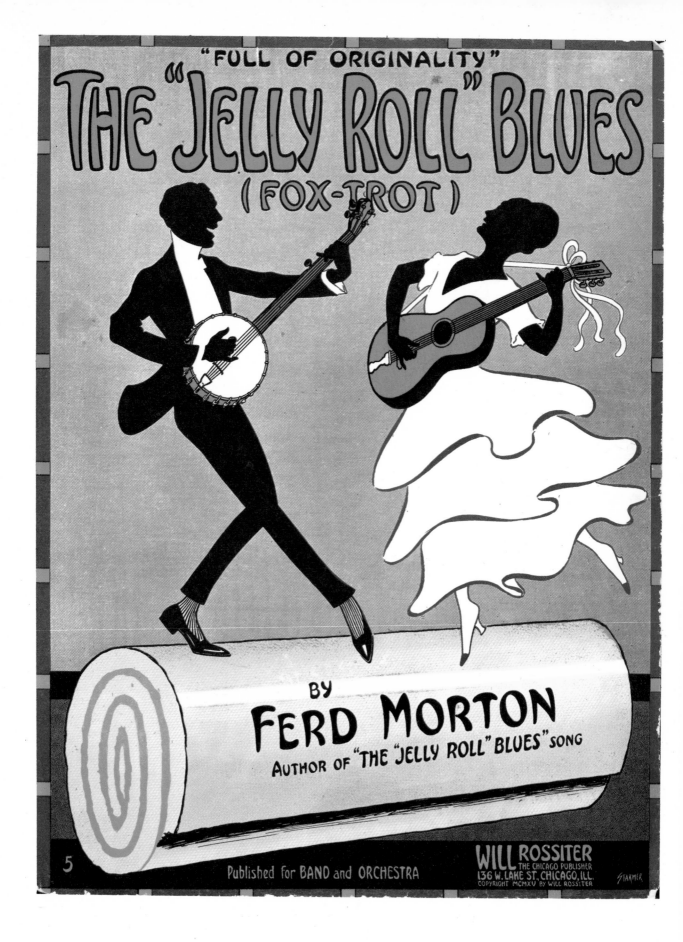

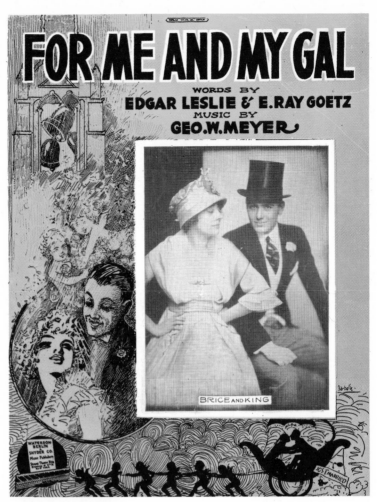

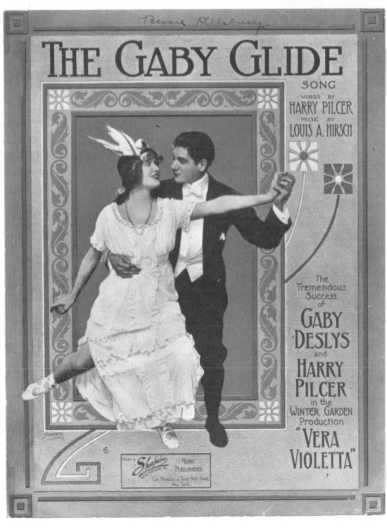

THE POLICEMAN'S HOLIDAY
1 or 2-STEP

MONTAGUE EWING

LONDON: PHILLIPS & PAGE, 5 Market Place Oxford Circus W.
AGENTS FOR AMERICA
THE BOSTON MUSIC Cº 26 & 28 WEST ST BOSTON MASS.
G. SCHIRMER, NEW YORK.
Printed in Great Britain.

COPYRIGHT MCMXI
BY PHILLIPS & PAGE.

PIANO SOLO   2/ NETT
PIANO DUET   2/
BANJO & PIANO 2/
ORCHESTRA   1/6
SEPTETT
MILITARY BAND 3/
BRASS   1/6

AS PLAYED BY ALL THE LEADING ORCHESTRAS

"TRÈS MOUTARDE."
(Too Much Mustard)
One or Two-Step
or Tango

By
CECIL MACKLIN.

COPYRIGHT MCMXI
BY CARY & Cº

PIANO   .50
ORCHESTRA Ten and Piano NET.75
SONG   .50

LONDON
CARY & Cº

NEW YORK
EDWARD SCHUBERTH & Cº
11 EAST 22ND ST.

ROW ROW ROW

INTRODUCED · BY · ELIZABETH BRICE

WORDS · BY · WILLIAM · JEROME

MUSIC · BY · JIMMIE · V · MONACO

ZIEGFELD FOLLIES

STAGED BY JULIAN MITCHELL

HARRY VON TILZER
MUSIC PUBLISHING CO.

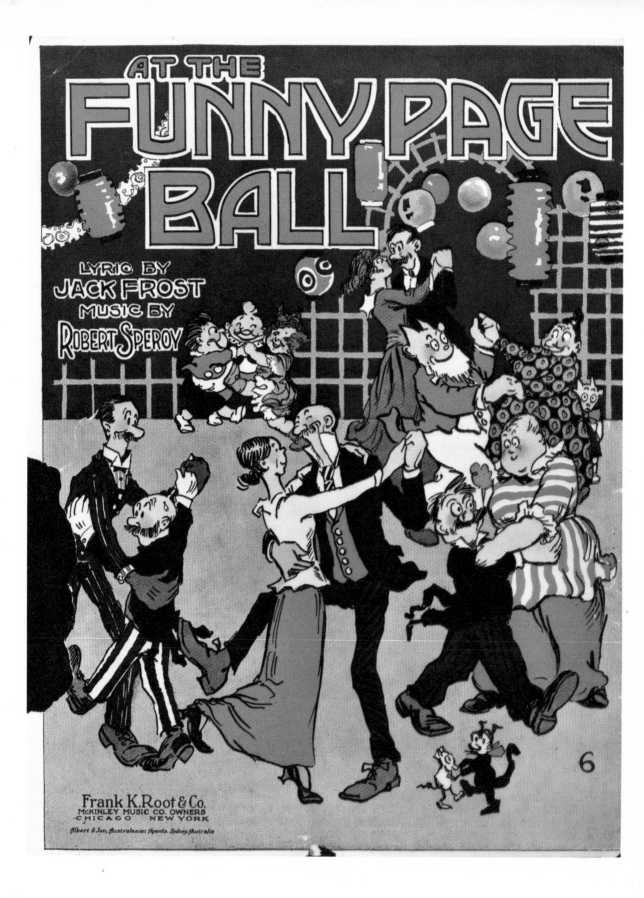

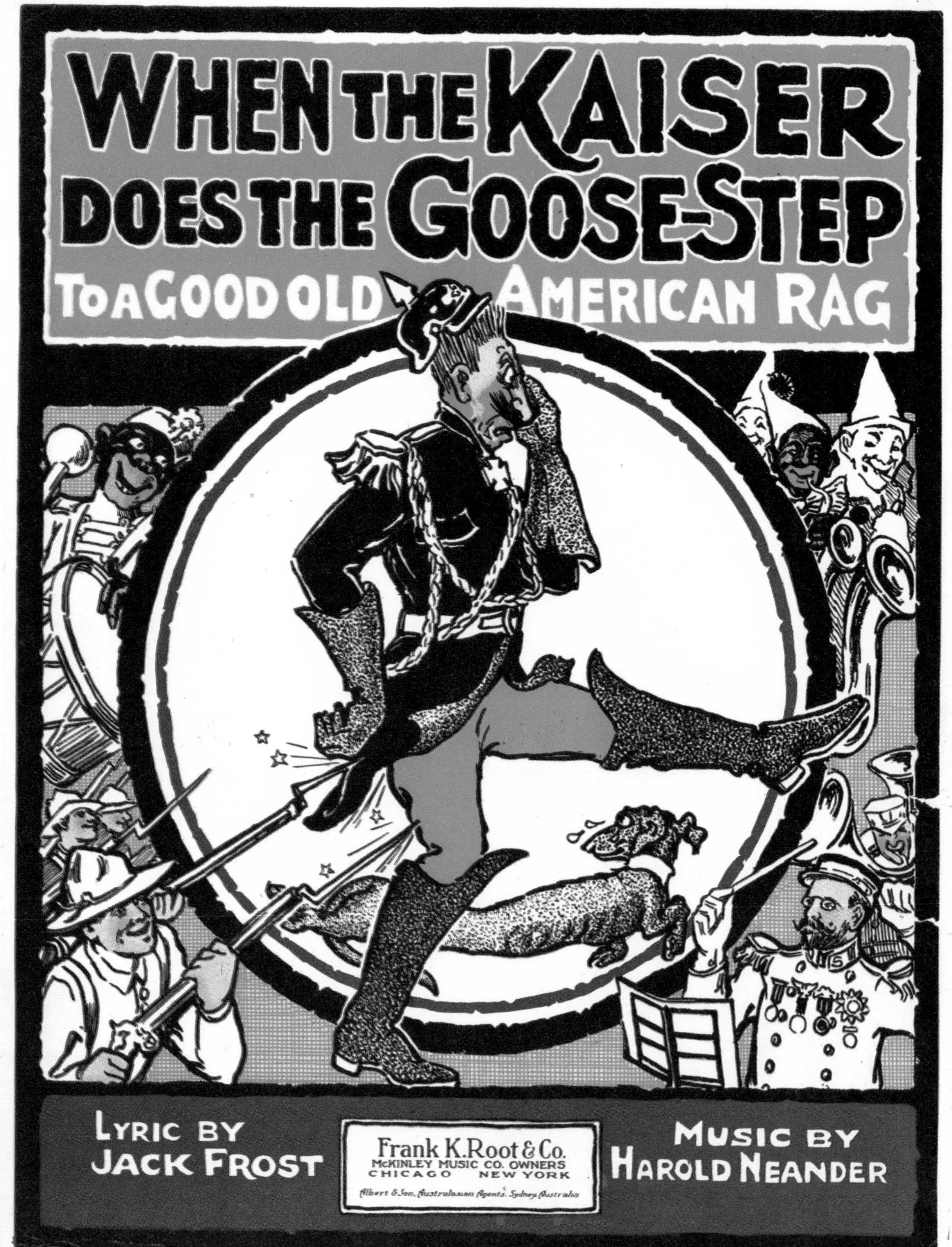
WHEN THE KAISER DOES THE GOOSE-STEP
TO A GOOD OLD AMERICAN RAG
LYRIC BY JACK FROST
Frank K. Root & Co.
McKINLEY MUSIC CO. OWNERS
CHICAGO NEW YORK
Albert & Son, Australasian Agents, Sydney, Australia
MUSIC BY HAROLD NEANDER

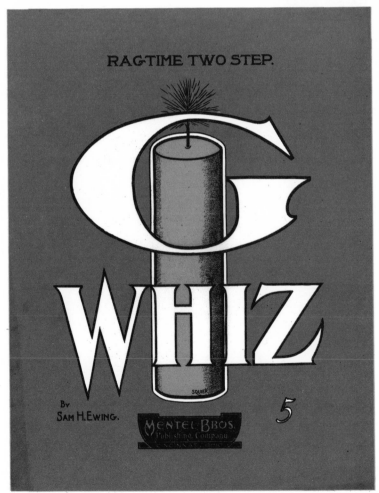

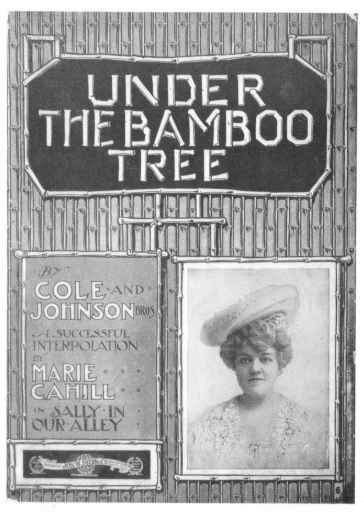

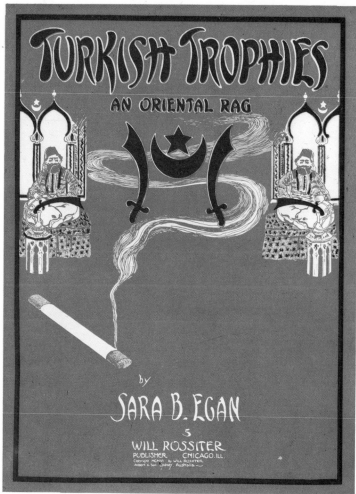

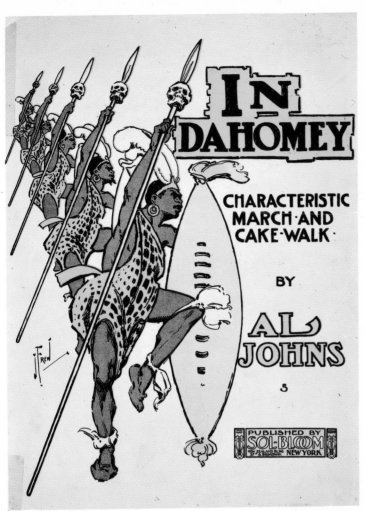

A NOVELTY BALLAD INTRODUCED BY EMMA CARUS
SIAM
Words by
HOWARD JOHNSON
Music by
FRED FISCHER
POPULAR EDITION
LEO. FEIST INC. NEW YORK
ASCHERBERG, HOPWOOD & CREW, LDT. LONDON ENGLAND

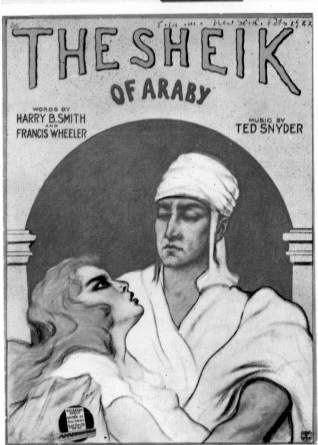

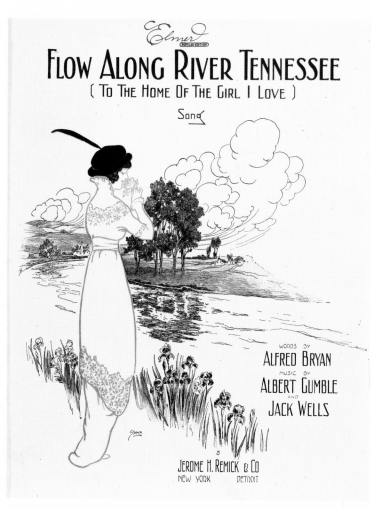

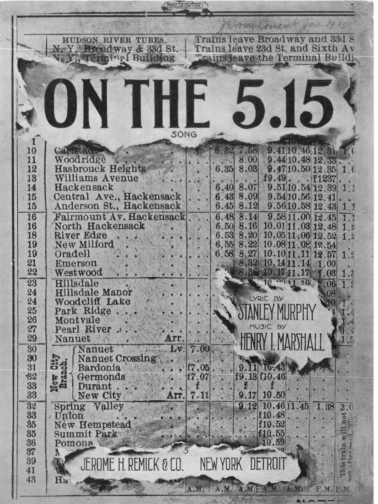

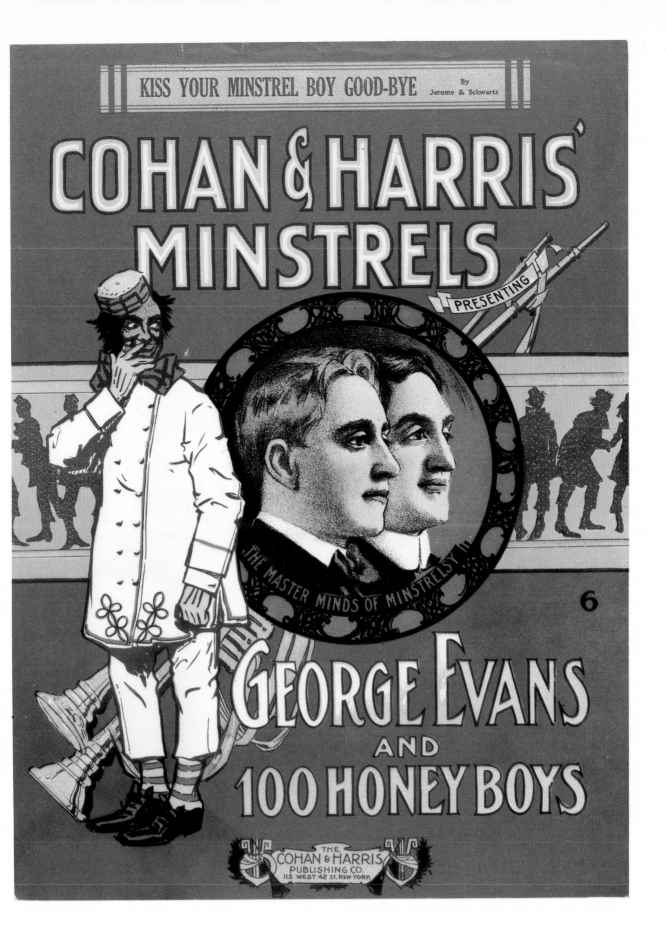

SHINE ON, HARVEST MOON

Sung by
NORA BAYES and JACK NORWORTH
in
"The Follies of 1908"

SONG
BY
NORA BAYES and
JACK NORWORTH

JEROME H. REMICK & CO.
NEW YORK   DETROIT

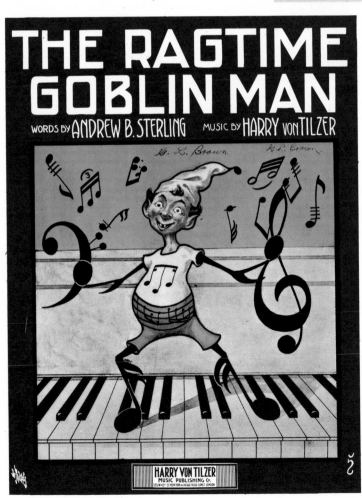

Inventory of covers

47 Row Row Row 1912
While many of these sheet music covers were designed by anonymous artists, this one was drawn by the late Gene Buck (1885–1957). Mr Buck, who was also a gifted songwriter (see *Hello, Frisco!*, page 78) wrote songs and sketches, and also directed, mostly for editions of Florenz Ziegfeld's 'Follies'. From 1924 to 1941, Buck was president of the American Society of Composers, Authors and Publishers (ASCAP).

48 At the Funny Page Ball 1918
Easily recognisable to comic strip afficionados over fifty are such American institutions as Andy Gump, Mutt and Jeff, Der Kaptain (and Der Katzenjammer Kids), as well as (down front) the immortal Krazy Kat and Ignatz Mouse.

49 Scrambled Eggs 1913
Movin' Man Don't Take My Baby Grand 1911
Bert Kalmar, the lyricist (1884–1947) wrote this song with Ted Snyder, who was Irving Berlin's first publisher and collaborator. Kalmar was a vaudeville headliner whose dancing career was ended by an unfortunate accident backstage in Washington D.C. He was later to form a long and lasting partnership with the redoubtable Mr Harry Ruby. The team wrote many hits for Broadway musicals, but the fans of their work will always cherish them for a jolly ditty which was to become a classic theme song for their good friend, Mr Groucho Marx, namely *Hooray For Captain Spaulding*.

50 When the Kaiser Does the Goose-Step (To a Good Old American Rag) 1917

51 If He Can Fight Like He Can Love, Good Night, Germany! 1918
Hello! Hello! Who's Your Lady Friend? 1913

52 Good-Bye Broadway, Hello France 1917
'C. Francis Reisner', the lyricist (along with Benny Davis, who was to achieve immortality as the author of *Margie*), later migrated westward to Hollywood, where he had a long and successful career as 'Chuck' Reisner, the successful director of comedy films for Charlie Chaplin, Buster Keaton, Marie Dressler and Polly Moran, as well as many other early stars. It is pleasant to contemplate the hands-across-the-sea motif expressed in this cover's art work, on which General Pershing and Marshall Foch are (somewhat idealistically, as the history books later point out) clasping hands.
Just a Baby's Prayer at Twilight (for Her Daddy Over There) 1918

53 Liberty Bell (It's Time to Ring Again) 1917
Till We Meet Again 1918
Richard A. Whiting (1891–1938) wrote this song as a young man in Detroit, Michigan, where he worked as a 'demonstrator' for the Jerome H. Remick Publishing Co. He had so little faith in the work that he discarded the manuscript. Luckily, his secretary fished it out of the wastebasket and brought the song to Mr Remick. The rest, as the books put it, is history, and indeed, no history of World War I can be complete without a mention of this ballad. (See also *The Japanese Sandman*, 1920, page 67).

54 My Red Cross Girlie (the Wound is Somewhere in My Heart) 1917
We're Goin' to Knock the 'Hel' out of Wilhelm (and It Won't Take Us Long) 1918

55 When the Good Lord Makes a Record of a Hero's Deed He Draws No Color Line 1918

56 There's a Long Long Trail 1913
How 'ya Gonna Keep 'em Down on the Farm (After they've Seen Paree?) 1919

57 America I Love You 1915
Mayor James M. Curley of Boston, Mass, whose face adorns the cover of this somewhat chauvinistic work, was later to be fictionalised as the hero of the novel *The Last Hurrah*, which recorded his long and colourful, profitable (and controversial) career as the key figure in Boston politics.
Mirandy (That Gal o' Mine) 1919
Lt Jim Europe, who wrote this song with Lt Noble Sissle, and Eubie Blake led the famous 'Hell Fighters' band of the 369th US Army Infantry during World War I. It was the Army's first all-black fighting unit. When the much-decorated 369th returned to the US in 1919, and its marching music led the troops up Fifth Avenue, those who were there report that New York crowds went wild to the syncopated brass band beat of Europe's crack aggregation. No recordings of its sound, alas, exist. (See also *Castle House Rag*, page 61).

58 That Mysterious Rag 1912
59 Cum-Bac-Rag 1911
Silver Fox 1915
60 Frog Legs Rag 1906
Dill Pickles 1906
61 Castle House Rag 1914
G Whiz 1914
62 Going to Pieces Rag 1915
That's-a-Plenty 1914
63 Rigamarole Rag 1910
64 Nightingale Rag 1915
Carbarlick Acid Rag 1904
65 The Mad House Rag 1911
Oh That Navajo Rag 1911
66 Down in Jungle Town 1908
67 Big Chief Battle-Axe 1907
The Japanese Sandman 1920
68 Under the Bamboo Tree 1902
Turkish Trophies 1907
69 In Dahomey 1902
Sol Bloom, who published this song, was later to enter politics, and became one of New York's Congressmen, for which career he is, perhaps, better remembered.
Down Among the Sheltering Palms 1915
70 Siam 1915
71 Dardanella 1919
The Sheik of Araby 1921
72 Moving Day in Jungle Town 1909
73 Are You From Dixie? ('cause I'm From Dixie, too!) 1915
Jack Yellen has had a long and fruitful career as songwriter and creator of 'special material', primarily for the late Sophie Tucker.

He and composer Milton Ager formed a somewhat stormy partnership in the early 1930s. Such was the friction between their two personalities that the two men decided to go their separate ways after completing the score for a long-forgotten MGM 'talkie', However, another song was needed for the film, and it was needed immediately. Reluctantly, Ager agreed to go back to the piano one more time with his ex-partner. Yellen recalls that he was staring out of the window of his home as the car bearing Ager arrived. 'Well,' he said to himself, 'here comes happy days again'. A few moments later, the phrase he had spoken was somewhat revised and became the title of the team's final song, namely *Happy Days Are Here Again*. That work became an instant success, was adopted by Franklin Roosevelt as his campaign song, and has rewarded Messrs Yellen and Ager with copious royalties ever since.
Bandanna Land 1907

74 Flow Along River Tennessee (To The Home of The Girl I Love) 1913
Down In Dear Old New Orleans 1912

75 I Want To Be In Dixie 1912
The Darktown Poker Club 1914
Bert Williams, whose performance of his own works (see also *Nobody*, page 26) convulsed Broadway audiences, was a West Indian who became the first great black star of the American theatre. Some of his talent is still preserved on records, a faint echo of his genius.

76 Casey Jones 1909
On the 5.15 1914

77 I'm Going Back to Chattanooga Tennessee 1913
Oceana Roll 1911

78 Hello, Frisco! 1915
Going Up (You Start to Sway) 1917
To list the various works of Otto Harbach, one of Broadway's most prolific librettists and lyricists for four decades, would entail a long paragraph of credits. Perhaps the most interesting to modern-day audiences, however, would be the current musical revival, *No, No, Nanette*, which Harbach wrote in 1923, and which has been entertaining audiences ever since.

79 Kiss Your Minstrel Boy Good-Bye 1908
Is it possible that anyone who has seen James Cagney portraying George M. Cohan in *Yankee Doodle Dandy* needs to be told of the handshake partnership between Cohan and Sam Harris, which lasted for the life of both men?

80 Shine On, Harvest Moon 1908
81 Kewpie Doll 1914
Who Paid the Rent for Mrs. Rip Van Winkle? 1914
82 Where Did Robinson Crusoe Go With Friday On Saturday Night? 1916
83 Ballin' the Jack 1919
84 The Frisco Rag 1909
Ragging the Baby to Sleep 1912
85 'Another' Rag 1911
The Ragtime Goblin Man 1911
86 Alexander's Ragtime Band 1911

DATE DUE
